Stop Investing Like They Tell You

STOP
INVESTING
LIKE THEY TELL YOU

THE PRACTICAL GUIDE TO **OVERCOMING**

THE POTENTIALLY RUINOUS FLAWS

IN YOUR INVESTMENT PORTFOLIO

STEPHEN SPICER, CFP®

NEW YORK

LONDON • NASHVILLE • MELBOURNE • VANCOUVER

STOP INVESTING LIKE THEY TELL YOU

The Practical Guide to Overcoming the Potentially Ruinous Flaws in Your Investment Portfolio

© 2019 Stephen Spicer, CFP®

Published in New York, New York, by Morgan James Publishing. Morgan James is a trademark of Morgan James, LLC.
www.MorganJamesPublishing.com

The Morgan James Speakers Group can bring authors to your live event. For more information or to book an event visit The Morgan James Speakers Group at www.TheMorganJamesSpeakersGroup.com.

ISBN 9781683509059 paperback
ISBN 9781683509066 eBook
Library of Congress Control Number: 201791888

Cover Design by:
Megan Whitney Dillon
megan@creativeninjadesigns.com

Interior Design by:
Christopher Kirk
www.GFSstudio.com

Photography by:
Jillian Farnsworth Photography
jillianfarnsworth.com

Illustrations by:
Paul Farnsworth

Limit of Liability/Disclaimer of Warranty: While the author has used his best efforts in preparing this book, he makes no representations or warranties with respect to the accuracy or completeness of the contents of this book and specifically disclaims any implied warranties of merchantability or fitness for a particular purpose. The advice and strategies contained herein may not be suitable for your situation. You should consult a professional where appropriate. The author shall not be liable for any loss of profit or any other commercial damages, including but not limited to special, incidental, consequential, or other damages. This book contains the author's opinions.

For additional disclosures, visit:

www.spicercapital.com/disclaimer.

In an effort to support local communities, raise awareness and funds, Morgan James Publishing donates a percentage of all book sales for the life of each book to Habitat for Humanity Peninsula and Greater Williamsburg.

Get involved today! Visit www.MorganJamesBuilds.com

For
Jessica
&
Grey, Lyle, and Cass

Contents

"Doubt is not a pleasant condition,
but certainty is absurd."

—Voltaire

CHAPTER 1
Why Should You Care?

I am not a doomsayer. Although it may sound this way at first, I have no wish to be an alarmist.

I am merely an advocate of prudent asset stewardship. A decade in the investment and financial planning industry has left me concerned for the investments of my family, friends, and fellow humans. **I'm talking about the vast majority of investors and billions of dollars in the market.**

See, I told you I'd come off as an extremist doomsayer… but bear with me, and you'll see I'm not.

First, you must know it's not your fault that you and your investment dollars are at risk; it's the poor advice you've received. It's the poor advice everyone receives: the investment paradigms commonly taught in schools, preached over the airwaves, and whose proponents include more than one Nobel laureate.

1

See? Not your fault. It's hard to argue with such a compelling force. Who would be crazy enough to even think to question the dogmas preached by such highly-esteemed authorities?

…?

Hi. My name is Stephen Spicer.

I have dedicated my career to helping people understand this potentially ruinous reality and providing them accessible, affordable solutions.

Why am I putting up such a fuss? It can't actually be *that* bad… can it?

It's tempting to think that. I *wanted* to think that; it would make life substantially easier. I could follow the cookie-cutter solutions to which most people subscribe, continue to market my services in the same way as other advisors, and do very well for myself and my family. That path would have been much less stressful.

There was just one problem (at least, it started as one problem): I kept discovering issues with the traditional investment paradigm… potentially devastating flaws in the logic. As I made these discoveries, I adjusted the investments I managed, only to find another flaw.

After years of searching for better solutions to each of these problems, I reached a point where I felt my investments could better withstand unpredictable stress without compromising the growth of a traditional portfolio.

I sighed a breath of relief...

...and then looked around and realized nobody else had adapted. Nobody else was dedicating any time to challenging the traditional investment paradigms. They all just continued to argue about the same old inconsequential issues: which stocks will perform better tomorrow, the exact implication of a particular word uttered by the Fed Chair, or the residual repercussions of Donald Trump's most recent tweetstorm.

Who Is This Book For?

Financial advisors may read this (and I hope they do; it could help), but this book is primarily intended for the average to high-net-worth investor. It's for anybody with money invested in the market who cannot afford to lose a substantial portion (say more than 50%) of their portfolio's value for an extended period (like decades).

The investment reality I'll bring to your attention can be as harsh and unsettling as the childhood discovery that Santa isn't real... except with your life's savings at risk.

There it is again—that doomsayer rhetoric! I promise it's not. My logic is simple and sound. My concerns are real, and I'm confident that within a few pages, you'll begin to question your own portfolio make-up and crave better solutions, just like I did.

And don't worry. The goal of this book is not, in fact, to leave you feeling anxious and helpless. Apparently, my Spicer Capital blog posts on this subject were depressing many of my readers; I'm writing this book as a hope-filled response. My purpose is to present some specific potential solutions for you and your life savings.

How to Use this Book

I designed this book with various levels of investment savvy in mind, from the knows-absolutely-nothing-about-investing-that's-why-I-pay-an-advisor-in-the-first-place investor to the Certified Financial Planner® practicing professional. It is designed so that any concerned investor can find what they need to understand my points and discover some stress-reducing solutions.

- **If the only reason you care about investments is because you have some and want to make sure they're okay,** you should *read the whole book,* from front to back. You'll need to understand the basics I explain to best understand the potentially critical risks to your portfolio.

- **If you have a solid grasp on market basics**—stocks, bonds, diversification, and correlation—feel free to *skip to Chapter 3.* Of course, if you'd like a quick review, or if there is a concept you don't have entirely nailed down, they're all there for you.

- **If you have read and are familiar with my Modern Portfolio Theory concerns,** feel free to simply *review Chapter 3.* I would at least skim it, though, so those concerns—the real reasons you should care about everything else presented here—are fresh in your mind.

- **If you already understand the basics of alternative investments** and are just looking for the meat of this book—the specific fund-type suggestions—feel free to simply scan Chapter 4. You'll find specifics starting in *Chapter 5.*

There you go—you get to choose your own adventure!

Why Should You Worry?

What's so bad to warrant all this fuss? Well, the answer to that question has two major parts that together compound the risk for you and your investment dollars. The first has to do with our current global economy, and the second with the critical flaws in investment theory.

1. The precarious and unprecedented state of the global economy

Life in our modern era can create a feeling of general unease. This discomfort is justified; allow me to summarize some of the most pressing issues relative to your investments.

- As of this writing in 2018, the US stock market has reached highs only seen once before (in 1999. Not even in 1929 or 2006 were they this elevated). [1]

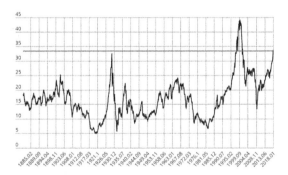

---

[1]   Explore the interactive infographic:
https://spicercapital.com/**cape-ratio**.
Source: http://www.econ.yale.edu/~shiller/data.htm.

- The bond market seems to be coming to the end of a massive bull run, and with current interest rates, its future does not look promising.

- Oh yeah, and interest rates: countries have *negative* interest rates now—crazy, right?! In fact, countries with negative interest rates now make up more than 20% of global GDP. We have never seen this before! Only time will reveal the outcome of this grand experiment. Sure, it could turn out fine … but it could also end badly—very badly—for anybody with money in the market.

- Interest rates in the United States are starting to rise, but they're still sub-2%, well below our historical average. Before the crash in 2008, rates were over 5%. Dropping the federal funds rate to near-0% was one of the primary ways the government attempted to spark a recovery. If the next crash happens within the next several years, that will no longer be an option.

Whether or not this information is new to you, these realities are important to keep in mind when considering the second part of this equation. After all, it's your asset allocation—and the accompanying promise that over any long-term investment time horizon, your savings will absolutely appreciate—that gives you confidence. Right?

It helps you sleep at night to know that, no matter what, 20 years from now, your investments will be worth more than they are today—isn't that what you've been told? If that's the case, you can easily stay the course, come what may. Bring it on! Am I close? Is that why these facts don't cause you to worry about the long-term viability of your invested dollars?

That axiom is precisely the problem.

2. The flaws in Modern Portfolio Theory (MPT)

Modern Portfolio Theory is supposed to protect you from these upsetting realities... but MPT itself is the second, more significant, problem in your investment equation.

What if that confidence were shaken?

What if you realized your confidence is derived from fallacious principles, and your sense of financial security is unsubstantiated?

What if, while dutifully following traditional investment advice, your portfolio could drop by 50% or more, and not recover within your lifetime?

If you were to discover that your 60/40 stock/bond portfolio is not the panacea it's made out to be, the aforementioned concerns become more real and more potentially ruinous.

Though difficult to stomach, I believe that's the case. Within a few chapters, I think you'll agree.

The Purpose of this Book

In view of our current global economy and the critical flaws in investment theory, I'm writing this book to present my practical, logic-based outlook, and provide some simple solutions that may better protect your portfolio without sacrificing long-term gains.

For you to best understand my case and subsequent suggestions, you'll first need to grasp the basics of investing.

*"The most difficult subjects
can be explained to the most
slow-witted man
if he has not formed any idea
of them already;
but the simplest thing cannot
be made clear to the most
intelligent man
if he is firmly persuaded that
he knows already,
without a shadow of a doubt,
what is laid before him."*

—Leo Tolstoy

CHAPTER 2

Market Basics

To understand why these alternative strategies might prove superior for your portfolio, you need to know why the professionals recommend what they do. Then you'll be able to defend your investment decisions—to others, sure, but more importantly, you'll understand them for yourself.

Stocks

It's important to understand stocks (aka equities), at least on a very basic level, because that's what everyone else around you (advisors, talking heads on TV, expert authors, your friends and family... *everyone)* is recommending to you. Stocks likely make up a majority of your portfolio today.

To grasp the risks of such high equity exposure, you must first understand how these assets function.

Stocks represent actual ownership in a company. Companies are divided into shares represented by stock certificates—physical pieces of paper that say you are part owner of so-and-so company. Today, because trading is so fast and frequent, everything is tracked digitally (although a company is still required to send certificates if requested). Your actual ownership is just a number digitally logged somewhere.

A super basic example of stock ownership

If you were to start your own company (or if you outright own a company now) you own 100% of that company's shares—there may be only one share, but you own it!

If you decided to bring in a 25% partner, you would have to split the company into four shares—your new partner would own one, and you would own three. As the value of the company as a whole goes up, so does the value of your shares.

If your business was worth $1MM, each of those four shares would be worth $250,000: $1MM (company valuation) divided by four (shares  outstanding). If, over time, the value of the company rose to $2MM, each share would be worth $500,000. You get the idea.

When would a company sell shares to the public?

When companies grow quickly, they often decide they need (or would like) additional funds to further facilitate growth. One strategy is to offer shares to the public. This is called an initial public offering, or IPO.

After a company's IPO, the shares of its stock are traded from willing sellers to willing buyers. That's where the stocks you own in your investment portfolio come from; they're all just shares in companies that have previously had an IPO.

So if you own one share of Amazon, you are, indeed, part owner of the company. Congratulations! Of its roughly 484MM shares outstanding, you literally own 0.0000002% of the entire company.

At this writing, Amazon CEO and founder Jeff Bezos  owns roughly 17% of the company. As his fortune climbs specifically as a result of Amazon appreciation, so does yours, relative to your actual ownership.

The opposite is also true. If, by some twist of fate, Amazon were to go belly up and wind up with a $0 valuation (I am definitely not making that prediction), the value of both your and Jeff's ownership would now be $0.

There you have stocks in a nutshell.

Bonds

Sometimes a company needs money but doesn't want to issue more shares to the public. Every time new shares are issued, the current ownership percentages are diluted, as those new shares must be stripped away from some or all of the current owners.

Consider our earlier example, when, in order to sell shares of your company, you went from owning one of one share outstanding to owning three of four shares outstanding. If you didn't want to go from owning 100% to only owning 75%, but you needed (or wanted) a cash infusion, you may have considered taking out a loan.

Most companies have debt as an option. Not only can a corporation take out a loan from a bank, they can also, in a way, take out a loan from the public. They do this through a bond offering. In exchange for regular payments at a certain interest rate, members of the public give these companies their money.

Now, like their stock counterparts, bonds can be traded from willing sellers to willing buyers. Each bond represents a regular payment and fixed value owed to the bondholder—whomever that may be at any given point in time.

A simple example of a bond

Let's once again consider your company. You and your new partner have a brilliant idea that you're sure will cause your business revenue to soar, but you lack the $100,000 you need to make it happen. You consider bringing on a silent partner willing to financially back this idea in exchange for company shares, but that would mean a reduction to your ownership once again. Reluctant to make that sacrifice and drop below a 75% stake, you explore other options.

Unfortunately, you find banks unwilling to finance your untested project.

You return to that prospective silent partner, motivated to make something work. You offer to pay her $5,000 every six months for the next 10 years, and then return the entire $100,000 principal. You're confident that by that point this investment in your brilliant idea will have produced multiples of that figure.

She considers that the money she keeps in her savings account is making less than 1% interest per year. Your offer of $10,000/year (a 10% return on her $100,000 investment) is pretty attractive. After much analysis, she believes your business idea will pay off and trusts you'll fulfill your obligations (i.e. pay her $5,000 every six months and return her principal in 10 years). She invests! Now you have the money *and* your shares.

You agree to allow her to sell this contract if she so desires over the next decade. In fact, it could be sold hundreds of times before the 10 years have expired, its price fluctuating based on the aforementioned considerations (current bank interest rates and public perception of your business's likelihood of repayment). You would simply make the ongoing payments and return the $100,000 principal to whoever owned the contract at the time.

At its most basic level, this is how the bond market operates.

There you have it—stocks and bonds—the simple building blocks for the majority of individual investors' portfolios.

Look at your investment portfolio

Really. Go pull up your portfolio. I'll wait.

So, what's your stock/bond allocation? 60/40? 70/30? 80/20?

Is your portfolio entirely derived from stocks and bonds?

Maybe you have 5-10% peeled off for other investments, like real estate or commodities. Do you think that's enough to mitigate the risks of being exposed to only two overarching asset classes (stocks and bonds)? Others exist, you know.

Diversification is a key principle behind MPT, yet most practitioners still advise you to invest almost exclusively in stocks and bonds.

Diversification

The importance of diversification and correlation are *critical* to understanding the inadequacy of MPT, so **make sure you get this part.**

The concept of diversification is encapsulated in the cliché of not putting all your eggs in one basket. The idea is that by mixing certain asset types together in your portfolio, you realize higher returns with less risk.

We don't have to get in the weeds of the math behind this for it to make sense.

An easy example of diversification

In the early 20th century, there were hundreds of independent manufacturers trying to succeed in the auto industry. By the end of the 1920s, it was dominated by Ford and GM.

If you had purchased Ford stock at its inception, you'd be doing great now. But what if you picked wrong and put all your savings on the

wrong horse—one of the hundreds of auto manufacturers who ultimately went bankrupt?

Enter the very basic need for diversification

What if, confident in the auto industry, but
unsure on which individual company to bet, you
simply purchased a little stock in every single
one of those hundreds of manufacturers?

Sure, you would have experienced a lot
of relatively tiny failures. The few long-term
successes, however, would have netted your
investment portfolio significant returns. Betting
on the auto industry as a whole was safer and
more profitable than attempting to divine the
winning horse.

Harry Markowitz, the father of MPT,
called this phenomenon "the only free lunch."
Through diversification, at no additional cost,
an investor can reduce her risk while also
increasing her projected return. *It's something
for nothing.*

Diversifying within an asset class has never been easier

Today, if you wanted to bet on the auto industry, you could find an Exchange-Traded Fund (ETF) that tracks an *index* that follows that particular industry. Investing your money in such a fund would be like purchasing a little stock in every single public company that operates within a respective industry or sector.

In fact, investors can utilize ETFs to diversify across most types of investments.

An **index** tracks a group of investments as opposed to just one individual stock or bond. The S&P 500 is probably the most familiar index in the United States. It represents the composite value of the 500 most valuable publicly-traded US companies.

Investing in an ETF that tracks an index instead of individual stocks removes the risk of a single stock going bankrupt and losing all your investment. It allows you to diversify across an entire investment class, like large US companies.

An ETF is a cost-effective way to do this. These funds systematically track those indexes, so they don't require an expensive manager or much in the way of overhead. Annual fees for ETFs go as low as 0.03%—that's 30 cents for every $1,000 invested. Super cheap!

If you invested in an S&P 500 ETF, you would own a small piece of each of the 500 companies that make up that index, and it would cost you very little time or money to do so.

Considering the thousands of companies in the United States and tens of thousands in the world, utilizing ETFs provides a cost-effective way to get greater exposure, spreading your risk. This diversification smooths your returns, making them more predictable and less volatile.

Lower volatility can do wonders for the long-term returns of your portfolio

Consider the returns over 10 years of the following two investment portfolios. Which would you rather have?

Portfolio 1	Portfolio 2
10%	6%
30%	6%
7%	6%
-5%	6%
9%	6%
-15%	6%
13%	6%
8%	6%
-4%	6%
7%	6%

Portfolio 1:

- Outperforms Portfolio 2 in seven out of 10 years
- Only has three negative years
- Its best year is up 30%
- Its worst year is down 15%

Portfolio 2:

- Only has a 6% return every year

If you invested $1,000 in Portfolio 1, you would have made just under $1,700 after 10 years. The same investment in Portfolio 2 would have yielded almost $1,800. This is just a made-up example, but the point is, although the potentiality for a 30%-up year and recurrent outperformance is thrilling, it is consistency, or **reducing volatility**, that is more important.

Why reducing downside volatility is so important

When you consider the amplified impact of negative returns, it isn't hard to see why Portfolio 1 underperformed in the end.

The damage done by periods of negative returns far outweigh comparable positive returns.

The dismaying reality of negative returns

Consider the fact that a 50% loss is much more impactful than a 50% gain.

Say you have $1,000. If your account goes up by 50%, you now have $1,500. However, it would only require a 33% loss to erase that $500 you just gained. A *50% gain* is counteracted by a mere *33% loss*.

If, instead, you start with a 50% loss, your $1,000 investment would decline to $500. It would now require a *100% gain* to earn back that $500 you just lost. A *50% loss* requires a *100% gain* to reverse its damage.

It gets worse—the impact is exponential. The bigger the initial loss, the greater the gain required to make it back. For example, a 90% loss (say, $1,000 dropping to $100) requires a *900% gain* to recoup your principal!

One of the primary goals of diversification is to minimize losses, and clearly, losses weigh heavier on an account than do gains. That's why it's so important your investments are well-diversified.

You can diversify within an asset class, like the ETFs we just talked about. **You can also diversify across various asset classes**—having some money in large company stocks, some in international stocks, some in government-issued bonds, and so on. This is where correlation comes in: it helps you diversify in a stable fashion.

Correlation

Understanding correlation can help you substantially reduce the volatility of your entire investment portfolio.

Based on historical data, correlation measures the degree that two assets move in relation to each other. This relationship is assigned a value between 1 and -1. This number is known as the correlation coefficient.

A positive correlation exists when assets move in tandem. If one goes down, the other goes down. If one goes up, the other goes up. The closer the correlation coefficient is to 1, the more in sync the assets are. For example, US and international stocks tend to maintain a correlation close to 1: when stocks in one developed country do well, stocks in other developed markets all around the world, on average, also perform well.

A coefficient around 0 implies little to no relationship at all.

A negative coefficient implies the assets tend to move in opposite directions—when one is up, the other tends to be down.

For example, stocks and bonds have historically displayed low correlation. In the past, their coefficient was mostly negative—they moved in opposite directions. Since 1990, however, bonds have tended to move in the same direction as stocks (a positive relationship), although they still maintain a low correlation (close to 0).

Incorporating uncorrelated assets in your portfolio can make your returns more consistent from year to year. As one asset class is down, another uncorrelated, or negatively-correlated, asset class might be up. This consistency reduces the portfolio's volatility, which, as we have seen, can lead to higher long-term returns.

This concept is fundamental to Modern Portfolio Theory.

"The greatest enemy of knowledge is not ignorance, it is the illusion of knowledge."

—Daniel J. Boorstin

CHAPTER 3
Modern Portfolio Theory

Today's Modern Portfolio Theory suggests that investors are served best by buying and holding a stock-and-bond portfolio using broad-based, low-cost ETFs to fund each asset category (large company stocks, small company stocks, government bonds, etc.).

Since stocks and bonds historically have a low correlation, the idea is that this combination reduces risks and smooths returns.

The Parts to Keep

MPT is great for many reasons. In fact, it is still the basis for a lot of my individual recommendations to clients.

Using low-cost ETFs (when possible) to achieve your desired diversification will save you a lot in fees over the long run, which can further boost long-term performance[2].

Even better, the buy-and-hold strategy employed by ETFs counterintuitively outperforms their actively-managed mutual fund counterparts. These counterparts, despite their active efforts to buy and sell stocks or bonds in hopes of outperforming the market, fail a majority of the time. And you still have to pay them for those failed efforts—often more than 1% annually, which is much more than typical ETF fees.

I agree with the many financial pundits who say that MPT provides a solid foundation upon which to build a portfolio, i.e. utilizing low-cost ETFs whenever they're available to fund each part of your asset allocation.

If your advisor is pushing you into expensive mutual funds for your basic US stock exposure, get a new advisor! It's possible to satisfy that allocation with an ETF charging less than a twentieth of one percent.

---

2 Explore these two infographics charting the devastating impact of high fees: "The Destructive Power of Fees" at https://spicercapital.com/**fees-destroy** and "The Negative Impact of Fees" at https://spicercapital.com/**fees-kill**.

I see a problem, however, when experts, pundits, and advisors tout a simple stock-and-bond-only portfolio as the obvious solution.

The Parts that Could Get You into Trouble

1. The Times, They Are a-Changin'

Many asset classes—including international stocks, investment grade bonds, US high-yield bonds, real estate investment trusts, and even commodities—have become increasingly correlated to the S&P 500 since the 2008 financial crisis.

Although bonds are historically the most uncorrelated to the S&P 500 Index of the aforementioned asset classes, they should not be the only other asset class used to diversify your portfolio.

A bad time for bonds?

Bonds have been a welcome addition over the last several decades, as they have been in a raging bull run (to the extent a relatively tame bond bull can rage), averaging more than 5% per annum. This has correlated with the gradual and extended decline in interest rates since the 1980s: in other words, interest rates and bonds are negatively correlated.

When interest rates go up, bonds do poorly. Interest rates go down, and bonds do well. We've already discussed the fact that, today, interest rates are relatively close to 0%. Last time they were this low, the following decades did not bode well for bondholder returns.

Consider the decades before our current bull run began. From 1953 to 1981, as interest rates rose from roughly 1% to almost 20%[3] bonds averaged an annual return of only 0.2%.

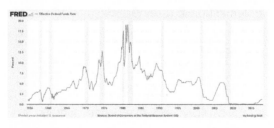

---

3 Explore the Federal Reserve data pictured in the chart or here: https://fred.stlouisfed.org/series/FEDFUNDS

I'm not suggesting bonds should not be in your portfolio. I'm saying that, because nobody can predict the future, and times and trends change, **bonds should absolutely NOT be your ONLY diversifier away from stock!**

2. Your Emotions Will Be the Death of You(r Portfolio)

Humans are emotional. Even if they have robots managing their money (robo-advisors), they still pull it out at the wrong times. Your emotions are the culprit!

The proponents of traditional MPT will tell you that the only way MPT works long-term is if people turn off their emotions and resist the temptation to touch their money. As much as we would like to believe we'll be able to do that, if history is any indicator, we won't. We can't. We are human, and our survival instinct leads to emotional decisions, which makes MPT fail.

This fact is well-researched and widely-accepted, yet we continue to invest in the same way, hoping we'll do better the next time the market crashes. (Are you starting to doubt the traditional approach yet? I haven't even shared the most glaring flaw…)

Dalbar conducts a Quantitative Analysis of Investor Behavior[4] every year. Their research demonstrates the difference between how investments perform and the returns actually realized by individual investors. From 1986-2015, the S&P 500 realized 10.35% per annum, whereas the average investor with similar stocks realized only an annual 3.66% return—that's the difference between $1,000 growing to almost $20,000 versus just under $3,000!

You may be above average (honestly, I'm sure you are, since you're reading this book), but that's quite the chasm to bridge. And if you really think about it, the above average investors who are diligently adhering to the principles of MPT might ultimately get hurt the worst.

In his book *The Behavior Gap*, Carl Richards summarizes:

The terrible irony in all this is that the people who are trying the hardest to stick

---

4   http://www.dalbar.com/QAIB/Index

*to their plans—the ones who hold out the
longest before they finally capitulate—are
the ones who end up getting hurt the worst
because they buy nearest the peak. Once
those hard-core holdouts give in, you
know the top can't be far away, because
there is no one left to buy.*

I would posit that the opposite is also true.
As markets free-fall, it's the "disciplined"
investors who hold out the longest—and suffer
the most—prior to their ultimate capitulation.

Consider the next crash

Maybe when the market is down 10%, we
can shrug it off.

At 20%, we remember the statistics we discussed above and decide to stay the course.

Perhaps at 30%, after calling our advisor
in a panic, we're talked off the ledge, and we
calm down.

But when the market is down 40, 50, 60%,
at some point, all logic and reason go out the
window. We know it will rebound again—prob-

ably soon—but that doesn't matter anymore: this is our life savings! It's too stressful to just sit back and observe. It is within our power to make it stop!

We decide to stop this pain, and we sell.

We get out and promise we won't ever subject ourselves to that unpredictable ride again. It's just not worth it—that is, unless we see others profiting from the rebound, and decide to get back in, well into the recovery.

Frankly, I understand. I would probably panic too if I had **so** much of my portfolio banking on the health of the stock market. This may sound contradictory, but *I think we'd be right to panic and get out!*

3. The 100-year Data Fallacy

If I had more than 60% of my assets broadly exposed to stocks, and the market started to crash, I would absolutely panic and want to withdraw my money. That's because I don't subscribe to the idea that the real value of the stock market must absolutely go up forever.

That's why I would never put myself in such

an undiversified position in the first place—60% stocks and 40% bonds, or any derivation therein, is simply not enough for the average investor.

What if what happened in Japan happens to us? Their market peaked in 1989, then fell 80% over the next couple decades, and today hovers around the halfway mark.[5]

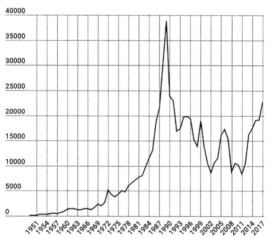

Japan's Nikkei 225 (like the US S&P 500) from 1949-2017. *Are we immune?*

---

5   Using the Nikkei 225 as "Japan's market" (like the S&P 500 is to the United States) https://www. bloomberg.com/quote/NKY:IND

Why should I rule that out as a possibility? The Japanese who listened to that buy-and-hold, stock-and-bond-only advice in 1990 got screwed!

Is it impossible to imagine US markets once again reaching the depths of the post-1929 crash? An 89% drop from top to bottom, and 25 years to get you back to even—and that's assuming you didn't touch your money (i.e. pull out and get in at all the wrong times, as humans are wont to do).

It may be difficult to imagine, given everything the "experts" are telling you, and the fact that MPT has proven reliable your entire life. But either of those scenarios, or even worse, are indeed possible.

Why?

Trends change, new realities happen, and history is made!

If you are within 10, 20, even 30 years of retirement, are you willing to take that gamble? Especially when I'm telling you there is a better way?

MPT creates a "damned if you do, damned if you don't" conundrum. Most people don't realize this, or even think about it, until the chaos begins. The market is dropping precipitously, and somebody brings Japan's history to their attention, and there it is, the conundrum: they could pull out and risk looking and feeling like a fool should the market correct immediately, or they could stay in like a "disciplined" investor, and risk the market staying below its halfway point or worse for the REST OF THEIR LIVES!

That's a tough call! I wouldn't want to be in that position, and I don't want you to be there either.

We don't have to be.

Although MPT provides us with a good foundation, the basic stock-and-bond portfolio is not enough.

We need something better, something in which we can be more confident, something that will soften the falls so our emotions don't take over. We need assets that are truly uncorrelated.

You need something that you—the individual investor, not just your advisors—understand.

If we can find all that, **we'll have much more confidence during our next chaotic event.**

*"We know from chaos theory
that even if you had
a perfect model of the world,
you'd need infinite precision
in order to predict future events.
With sociopolitical or economic
phenomena, we don't have
anything like that."*

—Nassim Nicholas Taleb

CHAPTER 4

Introduction to Alternative Investments

What Is an Alternative Investment?

The term "alternative investment" (aka "alts") is generally used to refer to any asset that is not one of the conventional investment types, such as stocks, bonds, or cash. Alts can be real estate, private equity, hedge funds, commodities... the list goes on.

Who Uses Alts?

University endowments make up some of the largest pools of invested assets, and since they have to publicly disclose their returns and allocations, they provide us with some amazing information.

Four of the five largest endowment funds have embraced an alternative investment strategy. Over the past couple decades, each has shifted their portfolio from an allocation very close to the traditional 60/40 paradigm to an alternative focus.

Those four university endowments are:

- Harvard ($32.7B)
- Yale ($23.9B)
- Stanford ($21.4B)
- Princeton ($20.7B)

The performance of these portfolios[6] over the long run has been nothing less than impressive. Over the last 20 years, Harvard averaged a 10.4% return; Yale, 12.6%; Stanford, 10.7%; and Princeton, 12.3%.

Let's compare the performance of those endowments with that of the traditional portfolio between 1997 and 2016. The S&P 500 Index[7]

---

6   Find more information about each endowment's makeup and history on their university websites or specifically at the following URL's: http://www. hmc.harvard.edu/docs/Final_Annual_Report_2016. pdf, http://investments.yale.edu/endowment-update/, https://finance.princeton.edu/princeton-financial-overv/report-of-the-treasurer/RoT_2016_ROI_FINAL.pdf, https://news.stanford.edu/2016/09/28/stanford-management-company-releases-2016-results/ (listed in the order they appear in the text)

7   http://quotes.wsj.com/index/SPX

averaged 7.7% per annum, while the Barclay's Bond Index[8] averaged 5.3%. Thus, the traditional 60/40 portfolio had an annualized 6.8% return.

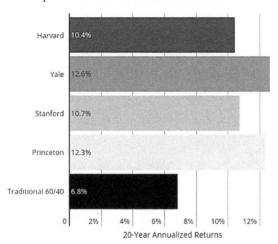

20-Year Annualized Returns

If you had invested $1,000 in a 60/40 stock/bond portfolio at the beginning of 1997, at the end of 2016 it would have been worth $3,756. If you had been able to invest that same $1,000 in Princeton's endowment, it would have been worth $10,078—**168% more!**

---

8   http://performance.morningstar.com/Performance/
     index-c/performance-return.action?t=XIUSA000MC

How Were These Endowment Returns All So High?

It is not coincidence that each of the university endowments embracing alternative investments substantially outperformed the traditional portfolio benchmark. Let's consider their asset allocation, and how it differs from the 60/40 split traditional financial advisors recommend.[9]

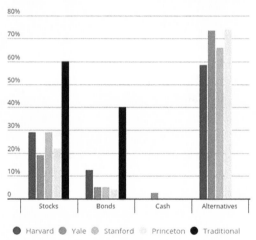

University endowment asset allocation. *Where do the best invest?*

---

9   Explore this interactive infographic at https://spicercapital.com/**alt-allocation.**

These endowments' outsized allocations to alternative investments have clearly contributed to their long-term outperformance.

These four universities are not alone

Consider the following statistics.

- The average pension fund[10] invests 27% of its portfolio in alts.

- The average endowment[11] invests 29% of its portfolio in alts.

- The average individual[12] invests only 5% of his or her portfolio in alts.

How does your portfolio compare?

---

10 According to Global Pension Assets Study 2016, February 2016, https://www.willistowerswatson.com/en-CH/insights/2016/02/global-pensions-asset-study-2016

11 According to the National Association of College and University Business Officers, http://www.nacubo.org/Business_Officer_Magazine/Magazine_Archives/February_2006/Pace_Yourself.html

12 According to the Money Management Institute, https://www.mminst.org/mmi-news/summary-2015-edition-distribution-alternative-investments-through-wirehouses

Much of this discrepancy can be explained by the fact that alternatives used to be inaccessible to the average investor. You could only find hedging and alternative strategies in hedge funds, and those are only available to accredited investors—individuals worth more than $1MM (excluding the value of their home) or making over $200,000 per year.

Today, however, *many alternative investment strategies are accessible and affordable!*

MANY **ALTERNATIVES** THAT USED TO BE INACCESSIBLE TO THE **AVERAGE INVESTOR** ARE NOW **ACCESSIBLE** AND **AFFORDABLE**

*"Blinding ignorance does mislead us.
O! Wretched mortals open your eyes!"*

—Leonardo da Vinci

CHAPTER 5
Advanced Alts

How Could You Gain Alt Exposure?

There are many types of alternative invest-ments out there—remember, an alt is pretty much anything that is *not* one of those conventional assets: stocks, bonds, or cash. Luckily, you don't need to know or understand all of them.

My "accessibility and affordability" claim is true for some specific alternative investment types, but not all. For example, private equity and venture capital are fun, sexy subjects within the alt universe, but they're still pretty risky, expensive, and relatively unavailable to the average non-accredited investor.

There are four alternative fund-types I would consider incorporating into your asset allocation strategy:

1. Long/Short Equity

2. Market Neutral

3. Commodities

4. Managed Futures

Long/short equity and market neutral funds utilize an investment strategy known as "shorting," which allows them to potentially profit during market declines. Commodity funds tend to move independently of traditional stock funds and work as a hedge against inflation. Finally, managed futures are relatively more complex— they offer a unique diversification that can thrive during times of market chaos.

Shorting

Before I dive into long/short equity and market neutral funds, you'll need to understand what it means to short. (If you already have a solid grasp on shorting, feel free to move on to the next section, *Long/Short Equity.*)

Money managers dedicate their careers to studying stocks. They determine most stocks to be fairly priced—not over- or undervalued—so they move on to the next one. Some, however, they determine to be mispriced.

- When they find a stock they believe to be undervalued, they expect it will rise faster than its counterparts, so they "go long:" they buy shares and hope for the best.

- If they find a stock they believe to be over-valued, they expect its price to fall faster than the market itself, so (*if they are allowed*, as is the case with these alt funds) they "go short:" they sell shares.

But "selling short" is not about selling stocks they currently own—that's just selling stock, not *short* selling. This is where it gets a little tricky, because they're selling shares they do not yet own. The investor is actually borrowing the shares from their broker and then selling them on the open market.

That leaves the investor with the cash from the sale, but also with an IOU—they must pay the broker back *with shares of that same stock* at some point in the future. In other words, they have to purchase shares from the open market to satisfy this obligation.

The whole point of "shorting" is that they believe the price of the stock will fall, thus allowing them to repurchase those shares (to repay their broker) at a lower price at some a later date, and pocket the difference.

For example: let's pretend...

August 7, 2015: I get sick after eating a burrito from Chipotle Mexican Grill. In my anger, I direct my broker to short 100 shares of Chipotle (CMG) stock at $749 per share. I've "borrowed" these shares from my broker and sold them on the open market. I've made $74,900 ($749 x 100), and I have an IOU with my broker for 100 CMG shares.

January 8, 2016: As I hoped, the price drops. I buy 100 shares of CMG at $414 each ($41,400) from the open market to pay back my broker. I profit $33,500 ($74,900 - $41,400) in five months from this "Chipotle short."

This strategy can serve as downside protection for your portfolio. If the market crashes, the short positions within these funds could be making money while everything tanks.

If the money managers have done a good job, the stocks of the companies they have chosen to sell short fall faster than their long positions—a profitable proposition. Thus, they have the potential—the structure—to make money under any market condition.[13]

Long/Short Equity

Long/short equity is an alternative investment created when funds sift the market, identifying stocks to go long and others to sell short.

Successfully run long/short funds reduce portfolio volatility. The ability to go short does not eliminate the possibility of negative returns,

---

13 Shorting is an important advanced market technique to comprehend. If you'd like to better understand what goes on behind the scenes to make this possible, check out Investopedia's video at https://www.investopedia.com/terms/s/shortselling.asp.

but it can soften the blow. Similarly, during
crazy bull markets, a long/short fund is likely
not going to capture all the upside return an
S&P 500 Index ETF would.

We've already talked about how reduced
volatility positively contributes to long-term
portfolio growth. Less dramatic highs and lows
tend to create a return schedule more like Portfolio 2 (in Chapter 2) than Portfolio 1.

On the following page, compare the performance of long/short equity funds during our last
two financial crises ($10,000 starting value).[14]

Even though these funds did not outperform the market in the recovery years (2003 and
2009), over the complete boom-bust-recovery
cycle, they came out ahead.

**They did this by managing their downside
risk**. They did that by shorting the weaker (or
overvalued) stocks in the market.

---

14 Data from BraclayHedge, LTD, https://www.
barclayhedge.com/research/indices/ghs/Equity_
Long_Short_Index.html

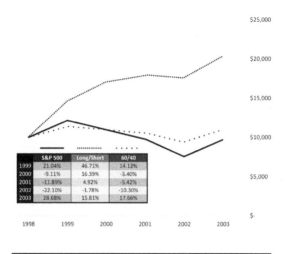

	S&P 500	Long/Short	60/40
1999	21.04%	46.71%	14.12%
2000	-9.11%	16.39%	-3.40%
2001	-11.89%	4.92%	-5.42%
2002	-22.10%	-1.78%	-10.30%
2003	28.68%	15.81%	17.66%

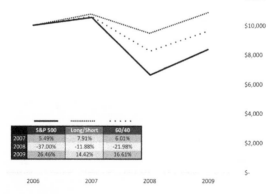

	S&P 500	Long/Short	60/40
2007	5.49%	7.91%	6.01%
2008	-37.00%	-11.88%	-21.98%
2009	26.46%	14.42%	16.61%

Market Neutral

Market neutral funds utilize a similar strategy, but with a different technique. Their mandate is to match long and short positions equally, in different yet similar stocks.

That sounds confusing, but it's not, really. I'll explain with an example. Consider again, Ford and GM (similar stocks).

A money manager is studying the auto industry. Each component of the industry—every individual stock, including Ford and GM—should move in relative tandem. Their correlation, however, will not be exactly 1-to-1. For example, if Ford stock went up by 1% over a given time, we could expect GM stock to move up a similar amount, maybe somewhere between 0.9% to 1.1%, but not necessarily exactly 1%.

If our manager determines that Ford is over-valued and GM is undervalued, both relative to the industry, he can go long GM (anticipating its share price will go back up to an average for the auto industry) and sell Ford short by the exact same amount (anticipating a relative decline back to the industry average).

The idea of this strategy is to emphasize the solid research and sound logic of good stock selection while **neutralizing the volatility of the market as a whole.**

Now, if the market has a crazy bull run and everything shoots up, the fund will profit in that climb, as long as GM goes up by more than Ford. During a downturn, the same logic would apply: every stock could decline, but as long as Ford drops by more than GM, the fund will achieve positive returns.

Market-neutral strategies are almost entirely uncorrelated to stocks and bonds due to their nature—and that's a valuable addition for low-correlation diversification seekers like us.

On the following page, compare the performance of market neutral funds during our last two financial crises.[15] Notice the relative year-to-year consistency despite market chaos and the impact that has on these funds' long-term returns.

By managing the downside risk of the market through shorting stocks, long/short equity and market neutral funds can help diversify and smooth your long-term returns.

Commodities

Commodities include cattle, coffee, corn, cotton, lumber, oil, orange juice, soybeans, wheat, gold, silver, platinum, palladium... the list goes on.

Historically, commodities tend to have a very low correlation to either stocks or bonds. And if we have learned anything from repetition, it's that smoothing our returns over time through uncorrelated diversification can afford us greater long-term returns. That is the entire premise

_____

15 Data from BraclayHedge, LTD, https://www.bar-clayhedge.com/research/indices/ghs/Equity_Market_Neutral_Index.html

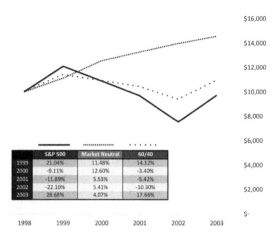

	S&P 500	Market Neutral	60/40
1999	21.04%	11.48%	14.12%
2000	-9.11%	12.60%	-3.40%
2001	-11.89%	5.53%	-5.42%
2002	-22.10%	5.41%	-10.30%
2003	28.68%	4.07%	17.66%

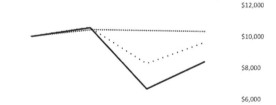

	S&P 500	Market Neutral	60/40
2007	5.49%	4.64%	6.01%
2008	-37.00%	-1.09%	-21.98%
2009	26.46%	-0.35%	16.61%

behind the very MPT most advisors and pundits embrace as gospel today.

Additionally, commodities are considered a great inflation hedge. Inflation suggests that the prices of goods are climbing. Commodities are an investment in the goods themselves, so if inflation were to go up, so would an investment in commodities.

With commodities, if skyrocketing inflation devastated your bond portfolio, you'd have a diversified position to help ease the blow.

There you have it. It's that easy. Another tool added to your belt to smooth your long-term returns.

Managed Futures

Managed futures generally represent contracts to buy or sell currencies, commodities, or pretty much any other financial vehicle at some point in the future. Historically, these funds are uncorrelated to stocks and bonds. They're structured to profit from rising or falling markets by utilizing those long/short strategies we discussed earlier.

Managed futures funds tend to employ trend-following systems unencumbered by human emotion. This unique structure, in my opinion, makes managed futures the quintessential alternative investment.

Most of these systematic strategies track one thing and one thing only: price. They don't care about how well Tesla's next car will sell, whether OPEC members will honor their oil output agreements, or how another country's experiment with negative interest rates will affect the value of its currency. They make trading decisions based solely on the technical analysis of market prices rather than an investments' fundamentals.

While everyone else may be panicking as the market enters a freefall, these traders are simply (and often profitably) following their systems and riding the wave.

That may sound scary and counterintuitive, but it suits our goal here beautifully—**uncorrelated diversification**. Not only are these strategies inherently investing in a broad range of asset classes (stocks, commodities, currencies, etc.), they're also utilizing a unique long/short strategy designed to offset some of the human behavior trends we see in the market.

When the investing herd frenzies or panics, moving any individual market dramatically up or down, these strategies stand to profit.

Consider how the average trend-following fund performed during our two most recent market crashes.[16] On the following page, notice how they thrive when the market is at its worst and the impact that has on these funds' total returns.

When you consider these results, and how uncorrelated this strategy is to everything else (and when one understands correlation and diversification as well as you do now), it's easy to see how this could be an advantageous addition to your portfolio.

Trend-following funds work as a sort of chaos hedge. And who wouldn't want a hedge against potential future chaos, like that of 2000 or 2008, or worse?

---

16 Data from BraclayHedge, LTD, https://www.barclay hedge.com/research/indices/cta/sub/sys.html

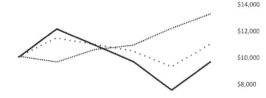

	S&P 500	Managed Futures	60/40
1999	21.04%	-3.71%	14.12%
2000	-9.11%	9.89%	-3.40%
2001	-11.89%	2.99%	-5.42%
2002	-22.10%	12.09%	-10.30%
2003	28.68%	8.71%	17.66%

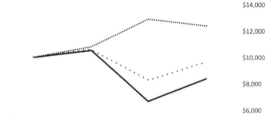

	S&P 500	Managed Futures	60/40
2007	5.49%	8.72%	6.01%
2008	-37.00%	18.16%	-21.98%
2009	26.46%	-3.38%	16.61%

*"Let every man divide his money
into three parts,
and invest a third in land,
a third in business,
and a third let him keep in
reserve."*

—Talmud

CHAPTER 6
Real Estate Investment Trusts

Technically, physical real estate is an alternative investment. Although I am an advocate of incorporating hard real estate assets into your portfolio (e.g. apartment buildings, storage units, and even land), that is a complex future book in and of itself.

In the meantime, investing in real estate investment trusts, or REITs, offers a decent place holder. There are a couple hundred domestic REITs to choose from, or a handful of reliable indices that track domestic and/or international REIT performance.

The managers of these funds invest in the industry they know best and the location with which they are most familiar. There are REITS specializing in commercial, industrial, residential, warehousing, hospitals, etc. in various regions around the world.

Owning ETFs that track REIT indices is likely your best bet for adequate real estate exposure. That will give you at least some degree of real estate diversification across sector and region.[17]

Consider the historical performance of the largest REIT index, the Nareit, during the 2000 tech bubble.[18]

	S&P 500	Equity REITs	60/40
1999	21.04%	-4.62%	14.12%
2000	-9.11%	26.37%	-3.40%
2001	-11.89%	13.93%	-5.42%
2002	-22.10%	3.82%	-10.30%
2003	28.68%	37.13%	17.66%

---

17   One big bonus of REITs is that every year, they are legally required to distribute at least 90% of their taxable income to shareholders in the form of dividends.

18   Data from the National Association of Real Estate Investment Trusts (Nareit), https://www.reit.com/data-research/reit-indexes/ftse-nareit-us-real-estate-index-historical-values-returns

The problem with REITs

I said REITs offer a *decent* placeholder. You may better protect and grow your assets through a diversified physical real estate portfolio. Unfortunately, that can be stressful and time consuming, and may be beyond the reach of most individual investors. Those interested in pursuing that level of diversification would be better served utilizing a financial advisor dedicated to understanding such investments—with Spicer Capital or another firm that recognizes the value of physical real estate ownership. So unless you are willing to take the time to learn the nuances of the real estate game (stay tuned—I plan to help with that in the future, for those of you who are) or hire an advisor to help, you should stick with REITs.

The problem is, as REITs have become more popular, and thus more heavily traded, they've started to behave more like stocks: the correlation between REITs and stocks has increased over this last decade.

The quintessential example of this is our most recent financial crisis. In 2008, with real estate playing one of the chief rolls in the crash, the performance of REITs and the S&P 500 was near lockstep: both were down roughly 37% in 2008, and both were up roughly 27% in 2009.

Don't write them off

That being said, over the last 20 years, REITs have been an incredible supplement to any portfolio.

If you had invested $1,000 in equity REITs from 1997-2016, your portfolio would have grown to $6,347. This same investment in an ETF tracking the S&P 500 Index would have been worth only $4,391. (Both figures do not factor fees.)

Clearly, REITs can enhance the performance and diversification of your portfolio—reducing risk, improving your odds of smoothing returns, and increasing your portfolio value long-term.

But don't forget, there is something even better out there. As your assets grow, consider hard real estate strategies.

"Everything should be made as simple as possible, but not simpler."

—Albert Einstein

CHAPTER 7
What's Next?

I hope the potential benefits of enhancing your diversification (with alts or otherwise) are clear. I sincerely hope you will take this information and put it to work in your investment portfolio—especially before our next financial crisis, whether that's in five months or five years!

I'd love to hear how your investing confidence increases as you take steps to better protect and grow your portfolio. But first you have to get it all set up—so what now?

Your choices run the gamut between handing it all over to a financial advisor, or opening and managing your own trading account online. Let's explore the three most common options: doing it yourself; using a robo-advisor; or hiring a professional.

1. Go It Alone

If you decide to manage your portfolio yourself, you'll need to set up an online account (if you haven't already) through a brokerage firm (e.g. TD Ameritrade, E*trade, Charles Schwab).

Simple asset allocation

You need to create your custom portfolio incorporating the investments with which you're most familiar, and then stick with it during the inevitable ebbs and flows. As you know now, the stock-and-bond-only recommendation from traditional advisors, although easy—much easier than selecting 10-16 uncorrelated assets—is potentially ruinous.

For those curious about or interested in pursuing this path—constructing and managing your own asset allocation—you should consider this book's Appendix an additional must-read chapter. It provides further considerations and a more comprehensive guide to designing your custom investment portfolio.

Resources

You'll have to research and identify funds to satisfy each piece of your portfolio. The mutual fund and ETF search feature on the *US News &*

World Report website[19] offers a fairly comprehensive overview of your options.

Warnings (potential pitfalls)

Pay close attention to fees.

Because the strategies mentioned in this text sound fancy, some firms charge the unsuspecting investor too much. Pay attention: be an informed consumer. Most of these strategies should not have fees over 1%.

Check the funds' listed fees. Usually that is sufficient, but (especially with managed futures funds[20]) occasionally hidden fees eat away at returns within the contracts. A review of your prospective fund's prospectus may be in order.

Read the fund's objectives as well. Be sure they have a mandate to invest only where you think they're investing.

---

19 http://money.usnews.com/funds/search
20 For additional insight reference Jason Zweig's January 27, 2017 *Wall Street Journal* article, "The Hidden Fees Inside Managed Futures Funds," http://jasonzweig.com/the-hidden-fees-inside-managed-futures-funds/

Rebalancing basics

After a year has gone by, your investment allocation to each category will have moved: perhaps small US company stocks will have gone up by 50% and now take up more than they were initially supposed to; REITs will have gone down by 30% and have less funds allocated than you wanted. You should fix that. Don't do it too often, though—once, and at the same time each year, will work just fine.

Rebalancing like this forces you to buy low and sell high—the annoying axiomatic advice that is near impossible to follow. By adhering to your self-imposed rules, you would sell some of those small US company stocks, your best-performing asset, while buying up even more shares in the REIT ETF, your worst-performing asset. You are buying low and selling high without even trying!

I'd love to continue to help you in any way I can

I sincerely appreciate you trusting me to lead you on this journey. I am humbled that you stuck around to the end. It is for you—the curious investor with an insatiable desire to find the best ways to protect your life savings—that I produce these resources.

It is difficult to cover everything in a book. The subjects covered here make sense in this format, but other topics are more fit for other mediums. For example, the specifics of setting up and running your own portfolio are much easier to understand when you can see my screen as I walk you through step by nuanced step.

To this end, I created a companion online video course. Find this free resource at https://SpicerCapital.com/**Course**.

My goal is to give you everything you need to invest your assets yourself. Whether you use it for that or to vet a financial advisor (or for family movie night!), my team and I will continue to create resources to help.

My hope is that these resources will make "going it alone" with confidence a realistic possibility!

2. Robo-advisor

"Robo-advisors" are software programs that trade for you. They make determining your asset allocation and keeping up with rebalancing easy and affordable (with fees often a quarter of what the average advisor charges). The most popular robo-advisor platforms are Vanguard, Charles Schwab, Betterment, and Wealthfront.

The problem is, as you might expect, they tend to adhere to the traditional investment paradigm. Check their suggested asset allocation. What is their allocation to stocks and bonds? How much is directly tied to a single country, i.e. the United States (yet another problem with traditional portfolios: being overexposed to the decisions of a single government) [21]? How diversified are their portfolios, really? At this point, you know what to watch for.

Knowing what you know now, how confident

---

21 This subject, although relevant, is slightly beyond the scope of this book. We explore this phenomenon and associated risks in the companion course: http://spicercapital.com/**course.**

are you in their almost-exclusively-stock-and-bond model portfolios?

Investing this way exposes you to all the concerns outlined in Chapter 3. A decision to "settle" for the predominantly stock-and-bond approach might work for a while… until it doesn't. That is to say, until the market begins to fall, and you remember my concerns. "Was he right?" you wonder. "Should I pull out now… or should I stay the course?" You become one of the tens of millions of investors who fall victim to the MPT "damned if you do, damned if you don't" conundrum.

But what other choice do you have, if you don't have the time or interest to "go it alone," and if you don't want to pay the higher fees (on average over 1% per annum) of a human advisor?

Introducing, Innovest

That's why we built our Innovest portfolios: to offer an accessible and affordable solution for the concerns outlined in this book. If the low fees and professional management of the robo-advisor option are attractive to you, be sure and include Innovest in your research. Find out more at https://SpicerCapital.com/**Innovest.**

3. Advisor

If you prefer working with a human, I understand—but be careful.[22]

At this point, you probably know more about alternative investments than most financial advisors. Do not hesitate to quiz them. If you discover you know more than they do, fire them and look elsewhere. If there are indeed turbulent times ahead in the investment world, you'll be glad you did.

You get what you pay for

The problem with working with the "best" advisors is that they tend to be expensive. Their

---

22 We've published several articles on this subject that could save you thousands of dollars over the long run. Use them as you make this important decision. Find them on the Spicer Capital Blog at https://SpicerCapital.com/**Blog** or more specifically at https://spicercapital.com/**category/challenge-financial-planning-paradigms/financial-advisors.**

fees follow the basic laws of supply and demand. There are so few highly-educated, original-thinking financial advisors that wealthy individuals are willing to compensate them well for their expertise. This often prompts these advisors to place a "minimum account fee" requirement on prospective new clients. This requirement can render the advisor's services prohibitively expensive for the average investor.

Fortunately for you and your life savings, **I believe most people can be empowered to invest confidently on their own.**

Whatever You Do, *Do Something!*

Everyone is different. Consider your options.

Want to "go it alone?" Great! You absolutely can. This book was a good place to start. Now go check out our other resources.

Rather "set it and forget it" (incurring negligible fees)? I can understand that too. Compare what each robo-advisory platform offers and find the one that fits best with your goals and investment understanding. Don't forget to work Innovest into your side-by-side comparison!

Can't ditch the idea of working one-on-one with a human? I get it. But no matter how much you like and trust them, with your life savings at stake, you'd better be sure they understand and have an answer for the critical concerns outlined in this book. There is comfort in having a culpable party other than yourself should the value of your portfolio crash, but surely the shield of the "ignorance" excuse is not worth your financial future. Do not hesitate to interview and evaluate different advisors in your efforts to best protect and grow your hard-earned assets.

Don't be complacent with your life savings.

Challenge the traditional investment dogma. Your future is at stake.

I wish you all the best as you build your new investment path and renovate your financial future.

Next Step

It takes a very special person to explore new and different solutions, and to accept the *possibility* they've been wrong all these years.

Clearly, you are above-average.

By completing this book (well, almost, the Appendix is important too), you've proven yourself willing to challenge the traditional investment paradigms to discover a better way to invest. *Congratulations!*

But don't stop now.

No matter what path you choose—go it alone, robo-advisor, advisor—we would love to help you however we can. We created a **free companion course** for this book. It dives deeper into several concepts essential to helping you along the way—including a few additional topics beyond the scope of this text, but just as important (for example, how to recognize the extremely common way advisors rip off clients, the flaws with most investors' international allocation, and questions to vet your advisor).

The *Stop Investing Like They Tell You* Companion Course offers several hours of video guides, comprehension quizzes, and a gamified learning experience.

I also have a special bonus for those of you who completed this book.

To gain access to your course and bonus, visit:

*https://SpicerCapital.com/***Bonus**

That's it!

Go to that site today, check out the first video lesson, and leave me a comment. I'll see it, and I will personally respond! I can't wait to see you inside.

I wish you all the best as you strive to better protect and grow your life savings.

—Stephen

*"The simple stock-bond mix
needs to be fine-tuned."*

—Burton Malkiel, author of A Random Walk
Down Wall Street

Intelligently Enhanced Diversification

Overwhelmed Yet?

I recognize this can all be a little overwhelming. A simplistic stock-and-bond-only strategy is much easier; I understand the appeal.

By this point, I hope you understand the problems and recognize the importance of finding a better solution. I hope I've provided you the information necessary to resist the apathy and laziness most investors experience, even after understanding these critical issues.

As with any difficult issue, it's always easier to follow the crowd—to invest the same as everyone else does, despite your newfound understanding. It's hard to be different—believe me, I get it. I've been there... I am there.

If and when that devastating scenario comes to fruition, it will be easier to throw your hands up in the air in frustration alongside the rest of the inculcated masses and exclaim, "How could I have known this was going to happen?"

As long as markets continue "business as usual," it's much harder to explain to everyone why you've invested differently. But if you wait until that explanation comes easily—say, after the next crash—isn't that too late?

I've experienced what you're going through: the feelings, the pressure, the doubt, the over-whelm. I was there, too, when I first started to understand these upsetting realities. Despite it all, I hope you'll persist. You will not regret it. Your long-term investment returns, your retire-ment, your estate, your legacy, and your loved ones will all benefit.

In fact, the path to overcoming the critical flaws in your portfolio does not have to be com-plicated. You don't have to implement immedi-ately all the strategies I've outlined. If you feel inundated by these new concepts and how to apply them to your situation, I want to offer you a step-by-step perspective.

At the very least, you should find ways to intelligently enhance your portfolio's diversification.

Intelligently Enhance Your Diversification

The core of diversification is investing across uncorrelated assets. A bond and a couple stock index ETFs are not enough. They can provide you with a fine starting point, but your assets will be better protected if you enhance that diversification in an intelligent way.

"Enhanced"

When I speak of enhancing diversification, I mean identifying and incorporating additional asset and sub-asset classes. A practitioner of Modern Portfolio Theory is likely well-diversified within a couple assets, but that's all. You could say they're a mile deep (via their index ETF exposure) but only an inch wide.

Ideally, your portfolio is a mile deep *and* a mile wide. As we discussed in Chapter 3, that is accomplished by investing across additional asset classes.

"Intelligently"

My use of the word "intelligently" is intended to convey the idea that:

1. Those additional assets you identified **reduce the average correlation** of your overarching portfolio.

2. You have a sound understanding of those additional asset and sub-asset classes.

Uncorrelated assets are the Holy Grail of your portfolio's diversification. They have the ability to increase your projected returns while also reducing expected risk. Remember the "free lunch?"

That being said, just because an asset is uncorrelated doesn't mean you should invest without further consideration. Specifically, if you don't feel comfortable with your current understanding of that uncorrelated asset or sub-asset class, you should not invest in it. A major part of an intelligent diversification is a sound understanding of your underlying investments. Otherwise, you're likely to prematurely pull out of an underperforming asset class after a year or two, simply because you don't understand its value to your long-term returns.

Start with what you know; add what you understand

Allow me to walk you through this process to get you thinking about how to improve your situation.

If you have money in a portfolio today, you likely own some stocks and some bonds. Hopefully, by now you understand those two asset classes and the value they add to a portfolio.

Can you diversify that stock exposure across a few sub-asset classes?

Most portfolios tend to be primarily exposed to the S&P 500. For some reason, it seems to be every portfolio manager's goal to match or outperform the composite returns of the 500 largest United States' companies each year. Again, I hope by this point you recognize that goal as short-sighted.

Do you feel comfortable with your understanding of small company stocks or international equities? If so, you should consider intelligently enhancing the diversification of your portfolio with index ETFs that track these sub-asset classes. Although these assets are positively correlated, because their correlation is not perfect (a coefficient of 1), this action should decrease the average correlation of your overarching portfolio. Great!

What about your bonds? Can you diversify that bond exposure across other sub-asset classes?

If you understand US bonds, I'm sure you can grasp the concept of and value in owning international bonds. How about different types of US bonds: e.g., Treasury Inflation Protected Securities (TIPS) or high-yield bonds?

Do you feel comfortable with your understanding of emerging markets?

No? Okay, no problem. Let's move on.

Or did you answer in the affirmative? Well, why not work them in too?

We discussed commodities. How do you feel about them?

If you have a good understanding of their value to your portfolio, why not dive further? How do you feel about investing in funds that exclusively track natural resources or precious metals?

What about real estate—domestic? International?

Did you understand how those alternatives from Chapter 5 work, and the value they add to a portfolio?

You get the idea.

Run through this exercise, taking note of all the asset and sub-asset classes with which you are most confident in your understanding of how they work and the value they bring. Identify 10-16 in this way. Statistically, after 15, the significance of additional diversification is dramatically reduced. So if your list is much longer than that, narrow it down to the ones you understand best, while maintaining a low average correlation.

It's Not "My Way or the Highway"

If your final list of asset classes does not include very many (or any, for that matter) of the new concepts I presented in Chapter 5, that's okay. Most investors have never heard of them before reading this. I hope I have at least piqued your interest in seeking additional understanding, as those alternative assets offer unique uncorrelated diversification. Perhaps over time, as your understanding grows, you'll feel comfortable working them in.

But even without alternatives, **I implore you to do something more than the traditional paradigm would suggest.**

The 7Twelve® Portfolio[23]

The 7Twelve Portfolio, created by Craig Israelsen, Ph.D., provides us with a perfect example of the value investors can realize from relatively simple improvements on the traditional model (read: intelligently enhanced diversification).

Israelsen's model portfolio spans seven asset classes incorporating 12 sub-asset classes.

---

23 **7Twelve is a registered trademark belonging to Craig L. Israelsen, Ph.D.**

7Twelve® Portfolio						
8 Equity and Diversifying Funds 65% of Overall Portfolio Allocation				4 Fixed Income Funds 35% of Overall Portfolio Allocation		
US Stock	Non-US Stock	Real Estate	Resources	US Bonds	Non-US Bonds	Cash
Large US Companies	Developed Non-US Markets	Real Estate	Natural Resources	US Bonds	Non-US Bonds	Cash
Mid-sized US Companies	Emerging Markets		Commodities	Inflation Protected Bonds		
Small US Companies						

Israelsen considers his commodity and real estate exposure as "equity-like." With that in mind, his portfolio is not far from the traditional 60/40 split—it contains 65% equity-like assets and 35% bond-like assets. Thus, the 7Twelve Portfolio provides us an example of relatively small changes and additions that can be made without straying too far from what you've been told your entire life.

He evenly divides his allocation across these 12 categories (8.3% directed into each sub-asset class).

Compare that to the traditional balanced portfolio.

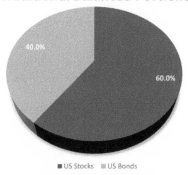

Over the last 45 years (many of these data points only go back that far), this portfolio has realized a greater annual return, while being exposed to less risk, than the traditional 60/40 portfolio. Specifically, you can compare those returns over the last 15 years in the following chart.[24]

7Twelve® Performance			
Calendar Year Total % Return (assuming annual rebalancing)	Passive ETF 7Twelve Portfolio (12 passively managed ETFs used)	Vanguard Balanced Fund (VBINX)	Vanguard 500 Index (VFINX)
2002	-0.76	-9.52	-22.15
2003	26.95	19.87	28.5
2004	17.8	9.33	10.74
2005	12.34	4.65	4.77
2006	14.96	11.02	15.64
2007	11.58	6.16	5.39
2008	-25.16	-22.21	-37.02
2009	25.64	20.05	26.49
2010	14.41	13.13	14.91
2011	-1	4.14	1.97
2012	10.64	11.33	15.82
2013	9.65	17.91	32.18
2014	2.5	9.84	13.51
2015	-5.07	0.37	1.25
2016	10.14	8.63	11.82
15-Year Average Annualized % Return	7.51	6.38	6.57
15-Year Growth of $10,000	$29,615	$25,299	$25,978
Annual % Expense Ratio	0.16	0.22	0.16

A $10,000 investment in either Vanguard fund would have been worth less than $26,000

---

24 Taxes and inflation not factored. **Past performance is no guarantee of future performance.** Average annualized return is a geometric mean, not an arithmetic mean. This information can be found at www.7TwelvePortfolio.com.

at the end of that 15-year period. Invested in the funds tracking the 7Twelve portfolio, it would have grown to just under $30,000—roughly $4,000 (or 15%) more.

For me, the historical outperformance is a bonus, but not my main objective. I contend that this intelligently enhanced diversification is better protected against the potentially ruinous flaws of Modern Portfolio Theory. I believe one can do even more, but Israelsen's model demonstrates the power of an intelligently enhanced diversification, even in normal market conditions.

In fact, Israelsen noted that it might be prudent to include additional sub-asset classes. Specifically, in a 2012 speech he gave at the University of Missouri, he commented on the prudence of including additional regional specific international diversification (i.e. Pacific and European).

The point of exploring the 7Twelve Portfolio is not for you to model its exact build out; it is to demonstrate the long-term value of incorporating more uncorrelated asset classes.

If you feel overwhelmed—if this is all just too complicated—don't let that get in your way. Don't feel like you must implement or even understand all of these concepts immediately.

But do something. Make some changes, even if they're small.

My concern is that if you do nothing, you are losing ground. Even small changes can have significant impact on your financial future.

Do something—anything—to move yourself in the right direction.

Acknowledgements

More than anyone, I want to thank my amazing wife, Jessica. When I told her I was unsatisfied with and wanted to leave my well-paying job, she was encouraging and incredibly supportive. Her patience has allowed me to build my business in a way I know will positively impact more people (versus making more money faster). Of the many lessons she's taught me, one of the most valuable has been to have the courage to challenge traditional paradigms when something doesn't make sense. Honestly, if it weren't for that critical concept, my business would not be what it is today—helping people invest *differently*. Instead, it would be just another cookie-cutter financial firm. Jessica, I cannot imagine life without you. You make me a way better person. THANK YOU!

My team makes it possible for me to put pen to paper. My talented property manager and good friend, Phillip Bentz, works more than full-time to keep my real estate interests thriving. And of course, my personal-Cici, Cecelia Austin, skillfully handles everything I don't absolutely have to do myself. Thank you both!

Mary Beth Conlee makes me a better writer every time we speak. I am fortunate and thankful to have her as my editor.

David Hancock and the whole Morgan James Publishing team helped make this process a breeze. I feel unbelievably lucky to have the opportunity to work with them.

The talented and artistic duo of Jillian and Paul Farnsworth have always been willing to help. J's skill with a camera is undeniable (jillianfarnsworth.com). Paul's drawings (you've seen a few) always put a smile on my face. I appreciate your love and support.

One more thing… is it weird to thank my boys? As I write these acknowledgements, Grey, Lyle, and Cass are only 5, 3, and 0, yet they inspire me more than anyone to create resources of which I'm proud—resources that have the power to help anyone (especially them, if something were to happen to me) better care for themselves and their families financially. Thank you, boys! I am sure over the years you will continue to bring out the best in me.

About the Author

After operating under the umbrella of a large brokerage firm, Stephen came to realize that his personal investment strategy was incongruent with what he was supposed to, or even allowed to, recommend.

He grew increasingly uncomfortable with the prescribed advice.

Unafraid to challenge the traditional paradigms of a broken system, Stephen built Spicer Capital to address his clients (and his own) investment and financial planning concerns.

His goal is to guide concerned investors and savers to their own educated decisions. That process may take longer and require a little extra mental energy than does following mainstream advice blindly, but their understanding and conviction will be much stronger. **They will be prepared, come what may!**

Anyone who knows him well will confirm: Stephen is driven by his growing family.

He married his brilliant high school sweetheart, and they have three amazing boys. His search for a better way to invest was initially inspired by his desire to care for them.

He hopes to be a resource for all who feel the same.

To learn more about Stephen and Spicer Capital, visit:

*https://SpicerCapital.com/**About***

Morgan James Speakers Group

www.TheMorganJamesSpeakersGroup.com

We connect Morgan James published authors with live and online events and audiences who will benefit from their expertise.